D0824787

HIP-HOP GREATS

BY STACY B. DAVIDS

Reading Consultant:
Barbara J. Fox
Reading Specialist
North Carolina State University

CAPSTONE PRESS
a capstone imprint

Blazers is published by Capstone Press,
151 Good Counsel Drive, P.O. Box 669, Mankato, Minnesota 56002.
www.capstonepub.com

Books published by Capstone Press are manufactured with paper
containing at least 10 percent post-consumer waste.

Library of Congress Cataloging-in-Publication Data
Davids, Stacy B.
   Hip-hop greats / by Stacy B. Davids.
      p. cm.—(Blazers. Best of the best.)
   Includes bibliographical references and index.
   Summary: "Lists and describes top hip-hop artists of the past and today"—Provided
by publisher.
   ISBN 978-1-4296-6502-5 (library binding)
   ISBN 978-1-4296-7247-4 (paperback)
   1. Rap musicians—Biography—Juvenile literature. I. Title. II. Series.
ML3929.D38 2012
782.421649092'2—dc22
[B]   2011002466

Editorial Credits

Mandy Robbins, editor; Kyle Grenz, designer; Eric Manske, production specialist

Photo Credits

AP Images: Jason Decrow, 10, Jerry S. Mendoza, cover (bottom), PictureGroup/Ben Hider,
cover (top); Danny Lawson: Press Association via AP Images, 26; Getty Images Inc.: Ethan
Miller, 14-15, Frank Micelotta, 13, isifa/Libor Fojtik, 18-19, Kevin Winter, 1 (bottom), Michael
Ochs Archives/Al Pereira, 1 (top), Redferns/David Corio, 24-25, Scott Wintrow, 6-7, 20, Tim
Mosenfelder, 23, WireImage for NARAS/Joe Kohen, 8-9, WireImage/EM/Kevin Mazur, 16-17,
WireImage/Lester Cohen, 4; NY Daily News Archive via Getty Images: Corey Sipkin, 29

Artistic Effects

Dreamstime: Miflippo

Printed in the United States of America in Stevens Point, Wisconsin.
032011   006111WZF11

TABLE OF CONTENTS

AIMING
FOR NUMBER
ONE

Great hip-hop artists aim to be the best. They write, rap, and dance all the way to the top. These gifted artists thrill fans around the world.

KANYE WEST

6

JAY-Z

(1969-)

When Jay-Z started out, record companies wouldn't sign him. So he and his friends started their own label, Roc-A-Fella Records. Now Jay-Z has more number one albums than any other solo artist.

sign—to offer a record contract
solo—alone; not part of a group

LL COOL J

(1968-)

LL Cool J started rapping at age 9. Def Jam Recordings signed him when he was 16. His powerful song "Mama Said Knock You Out" brought hip-hop to mainstream radio.

mainstream—widely accepted in society

FACT LL Cool J stands for "Ladies Love Cool James."

FACT *Speakerboxx/The Love Below* was one of the highest selling albums between 2000 and 2010.

OUTKAST

In high school, André Benjamin (Andre 3000) and Antwan Patton (Big Boi) didn't fit in. That's why they named their group OutKast. In 2003 OutKast won a Grammy for the album *Speakerboxx/The Love Below*.

Grammy—an award given annually for outstanding achievement in the record industry

MISSY ELLIOTT

(1971-)

Most hip-hop stars are male. But Missy Elliott didn't let that hold her back. She writes and produces her own music. Missy's songs are playful and confident. She is the best-selling female hip-hop artist of all time.

produce–to be in charge of putting together songs; someone who produces music is called a producer

BLACK EYED PEAS

Few groups score three number one hits on just one album. The Black Eyed Peas made this list with *The E.N.D.* Their hit single "Boom Boom Pow" was the most popular song of 2009.

FACT The Black Eyed Peas' song "I Gotta Feeling" has been downloaded more than 6 million times.

EMINEM

(1972-)

Fans love the way Eminem expresses raw emotion in his music. He is also an expert at making words sound like they rhyme even when they don't. Eminem has sold more than 80 million albums worldwide.

FACT

Eminem's song "Not Afraid" hit number one on the *Billboard Hot 100* the first day it was released.

FACT Ice Cube wrote his first rap at age 14.

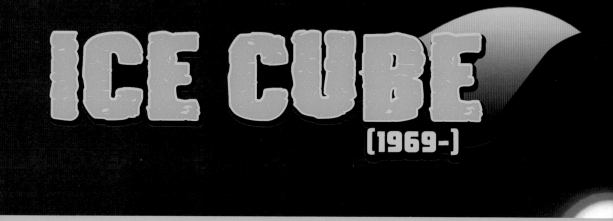

ICE CUBE
(1969-)

Ice Cube plays friendly characters in movies and on TV. But his raps are hard-core. He says his songs mirror real life. At the 2005 *Soul Train Music Awards,* Ice Cube won the Lifetime Achievement Award.

hard-core–a type of music with tough lyrics and a heavy sound

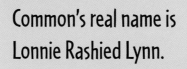

FACT Common's real name is
Lonnie Rashied Lynn.

COMMON
(1972-)

Common wants to inspire people to make the world a better place. He is known for clever raps about current issues. Common has won Lyricist of the Year twice at the *BET Hip-Hop Awards*.

lyricist–someone who writes the words of a song

KANYE WEST
(1977-)

Kanye West was a writer and producer for Jay-Z. After a car accident, his jaw had to be wired shut. During this time, Kanye wrote and recorded "Through the Wire." This hit song began his rise to stardom.

FACT Kanye won three Grammy awards for Best Rap Album.

NOTORIOUS B.I.G.

(1972-1997)

Notorious B.I.G.'s smooth voice impressed fans. At age 23, he was named *Billboard's* Rap Artist of the Year. His second album was called *Life After Death.* It was the first hard-core rap album to sell more than 10 million copies.

FACT Notorious B.I.G. died just before *Life After Death* was released.

DIDDY

(1969-)

Diddy is a hip-hop mogul. He is the CEO of Bad Boy Entertainment. Diddy produces and records music, creates perfume, and designs clothes. He also finds new artists and helps turn them into stars.

mogul–someone who is a powerful expert in business and entertainment

CEO–the highest position in a company; short for Chief Executive Officer

TUPAC SHAKUR
(1971-1996)

Tupac loved the fine arts. He studied acting, dance, music, and poetry. Tupac used these skills to become a hip-hop superstar. His record *All Eyez On Me* is one of the best-selling rap albums ever.

FACT Tupac's poetry is published in a book called *The Rose that Grew from Concrete*.

GLOSSARY

CEO—the highest position in a company; short for Chief Executive Officer

Grammy (GRAM-ee)—an award given annually for outstanding achievement in the record industry

hard-core (HARD-kohr)—a type of music with tough lyrics and a heavy sound

lyricist (LIHR-ih-sist)—someone who writes the words of a song

mainstream (MAYN-streem)—widely accepted in society

mogul (MOH-guhl)—someone who is a powerful expert in business and entertainment

produce (pruh-DOOSS)—to be in charge of putting together songs

sign (SINE)—when a company offers a recording contract to an artist or group of artists

solo (SOH-loh)—alone; not part of a group

READ MORE

Cornish, Melanie J. *The History of Hip Hop.* Crabtree Contact. New York: Crabtree Pub., 2009.

Gaines, Ann Graham, and Reggie Majors. *The Hip-Hop Scene: the Stars, the Fans, the Music.* The Music Scene. Berkeley Heights, N.J.: Enslow, 2010.

Weicker, Gretchen. *Kanye West: Hip-Hop Star.* Hot Celebrity Biographies. Berkeley Heights, N.J.: Enslow Publishers, 2009.

INTERNET SITES

FactHound offers a safe, fun way to find Internet sites related to this book. All of the sites on FactHound have been researched by our staff.

Here's all you do:

Visit *www.facthound.com*

Type in this code: 9781429665025

Super-cool stuff!

Check out projects, games and lots more at
www.capstonekids.com

INDEX